To God be all Glory, for all the great things He has done!

I dedicate this book to a special boy. I enjoyed working with him to improve his behavior and reach his goals daily. There were days when I thought he was getting too attached to me, until one day I realized it was the opposite. He taught me how to pay attention to details, how to understand the people I interact with every day and how look beyond the "label." My prayer is that he grows up and rise above every

negative comment anyone has ever placed over his life. I believe that one day he will be the best version of himself or fulfil the purpose for which he was created.

Jeremiah 1:4 KJV

"Then the word of the Lord came to me, saying:
"Before I formed you in the womb I knew you; Before you were born I sanctified you; I ordained you a prophet to the nations."

This is also to my husband James McCants and my Pastor/Spiritual dad James L. Pressey of the True Worship of Christ. In many ways you both are different, but you both always say to me "you can do it." Thank you both for always listening to my dreams and for believing in them with me. My children Raynel, Jordan and Josiah, thank you for being patient with mommy while I'm working diligently on my many dreams. To my grandma, mother, aunt, all my closest family and friends, who take the time to listen to me vent about my dreams and, most importantly, my purpose. THANK YOU from the bottom of my heart. My TWCC family, you guys believed in me more than I believed in myself. THANK YOU! My Brooklyn Dreams (where dreams become reality) family, for those I shared my journey with, THANK YOU! I pray the windows of Heaven open on you and shower you with many of life's blessings.

To my readers:

May this book inspire you to look beyond the children or adults you interact with daily. We may not get an opportunity to speak to someone for hours to find out the details about them, but let every second count. Even if it is just by saying "hello," let that hello come from the heart. Remember, every person has a purpose attached to them!

"What about Jeremiah?"

The one that you're not focused on, is the one that can tell you the entire show.

Written and Illustrated by:
Rayann McCants

Have you seen him? Did you notice him? He made noise in the crowd and stood—up unannounced. How did you not notice him? He was so loud everyone was annoyed.

In the blank boxes or circles you can draw whatever you think the author is trying to say.

Don't you remember that morning in the winter? I'm not making this up. He spoke over me while I was reading. His voice was non-stop!

He gets extra attention for doing not-so-good stuff. People come and get him all day. Boy, he has luck. I do my work and make no noise, but his parents visit you, and mine—not so much.

It's obvious all of you care for him more.

Jealous?

No, I'm not jealous, but you act like you don't see all the no-good stuff.

Should I run around the class? Walk in and out of the room? Would you notice me then or put me out of the school?

I think he's weird. Why, you say? He's quiet in the morning; by lunch he's fighting karate in space, by snack he runs around the class as though it were a track. You still don't notice, because your focus is on the class.

But I see everything, because
you seated me in the back.

It's not fair. I wish he would go; it wouldn't matter where. He's just always stealing the show.

School is almost over and the summer is near. I can't wait. I smell fun in the air.

I have plans to ride my bike every day, go to my nana's and have my own way.

I'll ask Mom and Dad to take me to Coney Island; I'm sure they'll say 'yes,' my report card looks final.

The fireworks show at Fourth of July is my favorite. We see it once a year and it's extraordinarily amazing. I can't wait for school to be out.

I'm tired of Jeremiah's mouth.

Mom woke me up this morning, and she said, "We're going school shopping today."

Wait,

Whaaaaaaaaaaaaaaaaaaaaaat!?

How did the summer go by so fast?

One day I was playing and then fell asleep.

Now I'm awake, mom, please tell me this is just a dream.

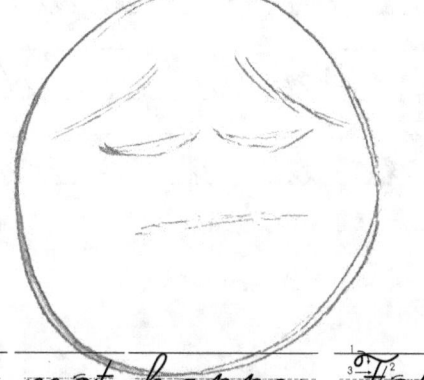

No, I'm not happy. For many reasons, of course. I don't want to go back to school, because of Jeremiah, the main source.

Don't you find it weird that school opens in the middle of the week? That's dumb to me, don't you agree?

Tomorrow is the first day. I can't wait to just get over it. I'm just not in the mood for none of it!

Oh, no.
   I'm late.
I better rush before Mom yell—
sings my name.

My foot touches the first stair,
and the school bell goes off.
This is it.
It's time to meet my new
teacher. I hope she's not a bore.

Mr. Spice was cool, but rumor
has it he left school.
I'm looking around the class;
there are a lot of new faces.
Maybe everyone else is in the
class where the teacher looks like
a space agent.

Soon it'll be lunch. I miss my other friends,
 except that one.

Lunch was fun. We played on the playground. I'm back in class, but,
wait,
I didn't see Jeremiah.
"Ms. Johnson," I raise my hand. "Have you seen Jeremiah?"

"No, I don't think I have," said Ms. Johnson.

What is this I feel?

Sadness, go away, please.

I don't like Jeremiah. I can't stand him. Why do I feel like crying for the boy that acts super silly?

The final bell rings, and I rush to the main office. "Can I see the principal, please?"

"Mr. Thompson? I was wondering, was Jeremiah in trouble today, and is he in your office?" "Oh, Raine, welcome back, but Jeremiah is gone." *Gone? What is he talking about? Is he in space?*

"Jeremiah went to another school, Raine."

But, wait.

Why?

I didn't mean all those things
I've said. I wanted some
attention in some sort of way.
But, I didn't get to tell him he
made me laugh every day.
I even wished I knew karate
good enough to fight someone in
space.

Weird, I know, look at my face!

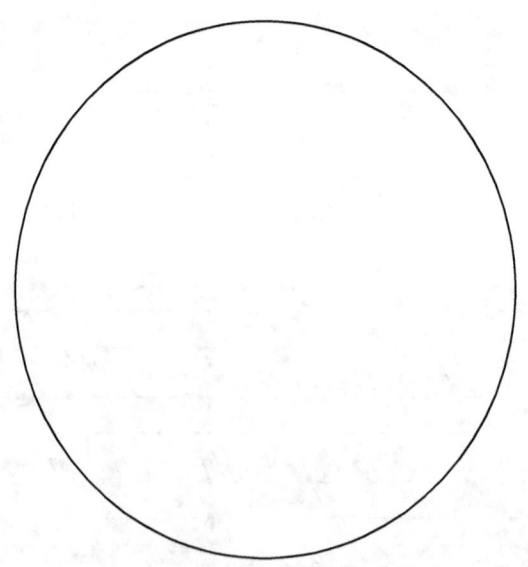

He was one of the smartest and most honest student I knew, He screamed everyone name, so they can feel special too.

$2^2 \cdot 4 = ?$

36×12

$2(x-1)(x-3)$

$\frac{1}{2} + \frac{1}{3} = ?$

Math is my worst subject and I got a lot of questions wrong. But when Jeremiah blurted out the answer, I quickly jotted them down.

I didn't get to tell Jeremiah I noticed him the most because I sat in the back every day, and that I wished I was pulled out from time to time by any adult, even if it was just to say, "hey"!

My heart is hurting. I feel it
in my eyes.
I'm not going to cry—not here
at least.
Sorry, tears.
Nice try.

So I won't ever see him again,
I guess. No one to disturb me
during my test.

I'll sit in the back and pretend
I'm in space.

I miss my friend Jeremiah. Don't you notice the sadness on my face?

It doesn't seem to bother anyone else. Everyone is happy and laughing.

But what about Jeremiah?

Books can be dangerous. The best ones should be labeled "This could change your life."

-Helen Exley